ABOUT TUTTLE
"Books to Span the East and West"

Our core mission at Tuttle Publishing is to create books which bring people together one page at a time. Tuttle was founded in 1832 in the small New England town of Rutland, Vermont (USA). Our fundamental values remain as strong today as they were then—to publish best-in-class books informing the English-speaking world about the countries and peoples of Asia. The world has become a smaller place today and Asia's economic, cultural and political influence has expanded, yet the need for meaningful dialogue and information about this diverse region has never been greater. Since 1948, Tuttle has been a leader in publishing books on the cultures, arts, cuisines, languages and literatures of Asia. Our authors and photographers have won numerous awards and Tuttle has published thousands of books on subjects ranging from martial arts to paper crafts. We welcome you to explore the wealth of information available on Asia at www.tuttlepublishing.com.

Published by Tuttle Publishing, an imprint of Periplus Editions (HK) Ltd.

www.tuttlepublishing.com

Text © 2011 Ann Martin Bowler
Paintings © 2011 Soosoonam Barg

Library of Congress Cataloging-in-Publication Data
Bowler, Ann Martin.
 All about Korea : stories, songs, crafts, and more / Ann Martin Bowler ; illustrated by Soosoonam Barg.
    64 p. : col. ill. ; 29 cm.
 Includes bibliographical references and index.
 ISBN 978-0-8048-4012-5 (hardcover)
 1. Korea--Social life and customs--Juvenile literature. I. Barg, Soosoonam ; ill. II. Title.
 DS904.B69 2011
 951.9--dc22
                            2010040845

ISBN 978-0-8048-4938-8
(Previously published with the ISBN 978-0-8048-4102-5)

Distributed by

North America, Latin America & Europe
Tuttle Publishing
364 Innovation Drive
North Clarendon,
VT 05759-9436 U.S.A.
Tel: 1 (802) 773-8930
Fax: 1 (802) 773-6993
info@tuttlepublishing.com
www.tuttlepublishing.com

Asia Pacific
Berkeley Books Pte. Ltd.
61 Tai Seng Avenue #02-12
Singapore 534167
Tel: (65) 6280-1330
Fax: (65) 6280-6290
inquiries@periplus.com.sg
www.periplus.com

First edition
20 19 18 17   10 9 8 7 6 5 4 3 2 1   1712EP
Printed in Hong Kong

All About
KOREA
Stories, Songs, Crafts and Games for Kids

ANN MARTIN BOWLER

Illustrated by

SOOSOONAM BARG 밝수수남

TUTTLE Publishing

Tokyo | Rutland, Vermont | Singapore

To Sarah and Jacob, who brought Korea home to us,
with love and thanks.

— A. M. B.

I would like to dedicate my paintings to all the people
who have made me who I am today.

— S. B.

Contents

Ancient Culture, Modern Nation

What's the spiciest food you've ever eaten? How do you break a board with your bare hand? Why in the world would you send a message off on a kite at the end of the year? Can Blue Dragons protect you?

Korean kids know the answers, and in this book, you'll learn too. You'll learn the foods Korean kids eat, the stories they enjoy and the art and crafts they make. You will learn games Korean kids play, the songs they sing and how Korean families celebrate holidays and birthdays. Some of these activities are fairly new but most are well-loved ways that have been around in Korea for generations.

Welcome to the rich and wonderful traditions of Korea!

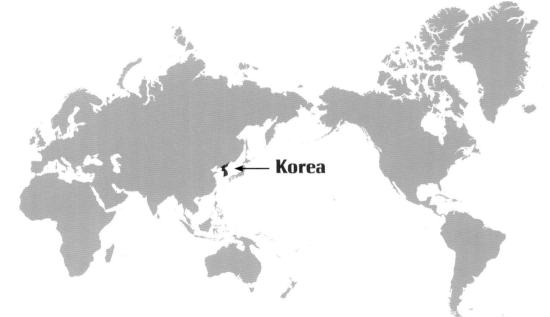

— **Korea**

Fast Facts

Country Name: Republic of Korea
Capital City: Seoul
Official Language: Korean
Population: 48,508,972
Total land area: 38,022 square miles
(98,477 sq. km)

Tallest mountain: Halla-san, 6,398 ft (1,950m)
Government type: Democracy
Money: South Korean Won
Main exports: Clothing, electronic products, fish, footwear, cars
Main Religions: Buddhism, Christianity, Confucianism

A Tough People Settle a Rugged Land

The first Koreans moved from northern Asia and settled in Korea around 5,000 years ago. These early Koreans lived in villages and survived by farming and hunting. Later, in the year 668, Korea became a nation.

With Japan to its southeast and China to its northwest, Korea often needed courage and strength to fend off its more powerful neighbors. Korea was known as the "Hermit Kingdom," because Korea just wanted to be left alone!

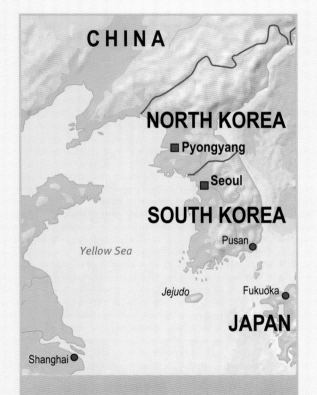

Korea is a rugged, mountainous country on a 600-mile-long (966km-long) peninsula. Korea has four distinct seasons. Summer is hot, humid and rainy while spring and fall are usually pleasant and comfortable. Winter is often cold and snowy, especially in the northern part of the country.

Being a nation for so long helped make Koreans a unified people. Koreans speak the same language, look fairly similar and share many of the same ways and traditions.

Over time, Koreans created ways of life and art that expressed their own special style. Beautiful temples and shrines were built.

In 1945, Korea was sadly broken into two countries, South Korea and North Korea. A wide military border was set up, separating the two. It became almost impossible to visit friends and relatives in the other Korea. That has been very difficult for Koreans, who dearly value family and friendship.

Though the governments of the two countries are still at odds, many continue to hope that Korea will be one nation again. Since 1945, the governments and ways of life of North and South Korean people have gone in different directions. **All About Korea** is about life in today's South Korea.

The Korean National Anthem
Ae-guk-ga 애국가

Donghae mulgwa Baekdusan-i mareugo dal to rok,
동해 물과 백두산이 마르고 닳도록,
Un-til the East Sea's waves are dry and Mt. Baek-du worn away,

Haneunim-i bo - u - ha sa u ri nara man se.
하 느님이 보우 - 하사 우리나라 만 세.
God wa-tch o'er our land for-e-ver, ou-r Ko-rea man- se,

Chorus Mu - gunghwa sam - cheolli hwaryeo gang - san,
무 - 궁화 삼 - 천리 화려 강 - 산,
Rose of Sharon, thousand miles of range a-nd ri-ver land,

Dae han saram Daehan - euro gi ri bojeonha se!
대 한사람 대한 - 으로 길 이보전하 세!
Guard-ed by her peo-pl-e, e-ver ma-y Ko-re-a stand!

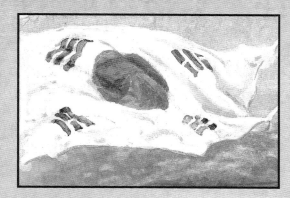

The South Korean Flag
Tae-geuk-gi 태극기

What does the South Korean flag mean? The blue and red circle in the middle is called **taegeuk**, "yin and yang." It means that everything has an opposite—like day and night, male and female, north and south—and it stands for the balance in life. The black symbols near each corner stand for the things that make up our universe: heaven, earth, water and fire.

Korea's National Flower
Mu-gung-hwa 무궁화

Koreans love the flower Rose of Sharon! Why? The sturdy **mugunghwa** can have thousands of blossoms, and it blooms all summer long. So it is a perfect symbol for the hardy Korean people who have worked together to overcome many challenges.

Korea Today

Hard Work Has Paid Off

In 1945, South Korea was a young but struggling nation. Years of military rule and war had left South Korea one of Asia's poorest countries. But the Korean people did not give up. They worked hard to make their country and government stronger. Koreans decided that education was the way to a better future. They built universities and insisted that all children go to school.

The hard work of the South Korean people paid off. Korea is now a world leader in the production of cars, ships, machines and electronics. Today Korea is very advanced technologically. Almost all Koreans use the Internet and have cell phones. The entertainment industry is also booming. Korean music, TV shows and films are popular across Asia.

With nearly 50 million citizens, Korea is a crowded country. Because it has so many mountains, its flat land is especially precious, and is used either for farming or for cities.

In the modern city of Seoul, the capital city, very old palaces and shrines sit next to tall apartment houses and skyscrapers.

Religion and Wisdom

Ancient Korean Wisdom

Even though Korea is now a very modern nation, three ancient belief systems still are important.

Long ago, Koreans believed that things like trees, rivers and animals were filled with spirits, and that some could communicate with spirits. This belief was called Shamanism. It is Korea's oldest belief. Though this old religion has faded, elements of it still exist in Korea today.

The Korean people are guided by the ancient ideas of Confucius, a wise Chinese man who lived around 2,500 years ago. Education and friendship are important in Confucianism, as is showing respect to your ancestors and elders.

Buddhism came to Korea in 372. Buddha taught that through meditation and living a simple life, a person can achieve a perfect state of mind called "enlightenment." Today, more than 7,000 beautiful Buddhist temples dot the Korean landscape and about 23% of South Koreans consider themselves to be Buddhist.

Catholicism arrived in Korea in 1794 and Protestant faiths entered Korea during the 1880s. Before long, thousands of Koreans had converted to Christian faiths. Today, about 29% of South Koreans call themselves Christians.

KOREAN PROVERBS
Sok-dam 속담

Though Korea is a modern nation, Korean parents continue to tell their children the same time-tested bits of wisdom their own parents told them. Why do parents repeat old proverbs? In the hope that their children will become dependable, compassionate, hardworking adults!

Blue Dragons & White Tigers

Long ago, Koreans believed Blue Dragons brought rain and controlled the seas, and White Tigers could change shapes and become other animals. Both were considered very powerful.

An old Korean saying, "Blue Dragons on our left side, White Tigers on our right side," is about the Korean belief that White Tigers protected Koreans from evils coming from the west and Blue Dragons protected them from the east. Koreans took these beliefs from an ancient Chinese philosophy called feng shui.

Today, most of Korea's 7,000 temples have Blue Dragons on the east side and White Tigers on the west side.

Taming a Tiger

Koreans feared and respected the tigers that once roamed their mountains. Here is one of many wonderful Korean tales about tigers.

"Jung, thank goodness you're home!" cried Ogi, rushing to her husband. "Come sit down. Tell me, is the war over?"

But Jung only replied, "Give me peace, woman!"

Ogi told Jung funny stories, trying to cheer him up. But he said sternly, "Enough, woman! Let me rest!"

Then Ogi decided, "My husband is too thin! Some homemade food will do him good."

But no matter what Ogi cooked, Jung pushed it away saying, "This bulgogi is overcooked!" or "This is too salty!" or "This isn't spicy enough!"

A few days later, Jung finally set off to farm their land. At first Ogi was overjoyed, but her happiness didn't last long. "My husband is worthless! Look at him. He just sits and stares at the sea! His body is home, but the loving man I knew is gone. What should I do?"

One day Ogi heard about a wise old hermit who made healing potions. She set out for his home right away. The old man answered his door gruffly. "What do you want?"

Ogi answered politely, "Wise One, I need a magic potion."

Sighing, the old man said, "What is your story?"

"My husband is not himself," began Ogi, her voice quivering. When Ogi finished her sad tale, the Wise One replied, "Yes, this happens sometimes when men return from war."

Encouraged, Ogi asked hopefully, "Wise One, can you make a potion so my husband will be himself again?"

"So simple, is it?" the old hermit laughed. But after a long while, he said, "This potion is most difficult but it can be made. The key ingredient is the whisker of a living tiger. Bring me a whisker and I will make a magic potion."

Ogi was astonished. "The whisker from a living tiger? Impossible!"

"If helping your husband is important enough, you will find a way," the hermit replied, as he shut his door.

"A tiger's whisker? I would be killed!" Ogi worried. But Jung did not improve, so finally, one sleepless night, Ogi took some rice and meat, tiptoed from her dark house and hiked to caves where tigers were known to live.

Standing far from the caves, Ogi sang in a shaking voice, "Tiger, sweet tiger, dinnertime!" But by daybreak, no tiger had appeared so Ogi left the food and headed home.

Each night, Ogi faithfully brought food and forced herself closer to the tigers' caves. She sang sweetly for hours on end, "Tiger, sweet tiger, dinnertime."

One night, a tiger seemed to be waiting for Ogi on the trail. Ogi was so startled she dropped the food. She shivered as the powerful animal gobbled it up.

From then on, the tiger met Ogi on the trail. In the dark, Ogi smelled the tiger's hot breath and heard him chew. She was delighted to see his tail swish when she sang, "Tiger, sweet tiger! Dinnertime!"

One night Ogi forced herself to reach out and scratch the thick fur behind the tiger's ear. To her amazement, the tiger purred! From then on, Ogi not only scratched the tiger's neck but petted his long powerful sides as well.

Seven nights later, while the tiger was enjoying her scratching, Ogi drew a deep breath and said, "Tiger, my friend, I need one of your whiskers. Please don't be angry." The tiger didn't seem to notice as Ogi cut off a whisker.

Clutching the whisker, Ogi ran straight to the hermit's house. "Wise One!" Ogi called excitedly, "I have a tiger's whisker! Please make a potion so my husband will be happy again."

The hermit studied the whisker sleepily. Satisfied it was from a living tiger, he dropped it into his fire.

"No!" cried Ogi. "Don't burn the whisker!"

The old hermit answered calmly, "Tell me, how did you get the whisker?"

"I brought the tiger food each night," Ogi said. "At first, I stood far from the caves. Each night I went closer, singing 'Tiger, sweet tiger, dinnertime,' over and over. I was tired, but I didn't give up. I went night after night and finally, finally, the tiger came to me. Soon he ate out of my hand and purred when I scratched him. It was then that I took a whisker."

"I am impressed! Through your kindness and patience, you tamed a tiger!" the hermit said warmly.

"I guess I did. But you burned the whisker!" Ogi said sadly. "All my work was for nothing."

"You are wrong. Your work was most important. The whisker is no longer needed," the hermit said firmly. "Ogi, come sit beside me. I need to ask some questions."

Settling in front of the fire, the hermit asked, "Who is more fierce, your husband or the tiger you tamed?"

"The tiger, of course," Ogi replied.

"If you can win the love and confidence of a wild animal by your kindness, could you not do the same with your husband?" the hermit asked.

Ogi was speechless. But then, with a smile on her face, Ogi thanked the hermit and raced toward home, thinking all the while of what she had learned from the wise old hermit.

A KOREAN PROVERB

Horangi gure gaya horangi-reul jam-neunda.
호랑이 굴에 가야 호랑이를 잡는다.
"If you want to catch a tiger, you have to go to the tiger's cave."

This is a well-known Korean proverb. It means: Work hard! You must overcome difficulties to achieve your goals!

Make a Korean White Tiger Puppet

You will need:
- White paper lunch bag
- Glue, scissors
- Black crayon or marker
- Wiggly eyes (optional)

To make it:

1. Draw your own tiger head and arms on paper, color them, then cut them out. (Or print out the template at *www.tuttlepublishing.com*; use a photocopier to enlarge it 200%.) If you are using wiggly eyes, glue them on the face.

2. Color black stripes on the paper bag to make the tiger's body.

3. Glue the head onto the folded "bottom" part of the paper bag.

4. Glue the arms into the side folds of the bag.

5. Slip your hand into the puppet. Wave your fingers to move its head.

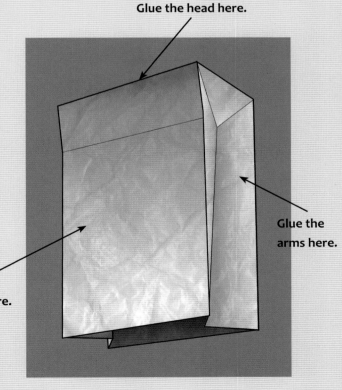

Glue the head here.

Glue the arms here.

Color black stripes here.

Great Games and Activities

Time for Some Korean-Style Fun!

Do Koreans enjoy sports and games? You bet! Traditional Korean pastimes include kite flying, tug-of-war, archery and **ssireum**, which is a Korean style of wrestling.

Today, South Koreans like many activities including hiking, skiing, board games like chess, and computer games.

Long ago, when most Koreans had little money, people created games using things they had around them, like sticks, paper or pebbles. So it's not surprising that most traditional Korean games are great fun but require very few materials.

Ssireum is one of the oldest of Korea's traditional sports. In the modern form, each contestant wears a belt that wraps around their waist and thigh. The matches are held in a circular ring with a floor of sand. The two contestants begin the match by kneeling on the sand face to face, and gripping onto their opponent's belt. The match begins as they stand up together, and the winner is the wrestler who forces the other to touch the ground with any part of his body higher than the knee.

Taekwondo 태권도

What is the best-known sport from Korea? It's **taekwondo**, a martial art known for its fast, high, spinning kicks. The roots of taekwondo began 2,000 years ago when Korean warriors developed a style of fighting that used bare hands and feet instead of weapons. The word taekwondo means "the way of the foot and fist." Today it is one of the most popular martial arts in the world. It has been an Olympic sport since 2000.

Taekwondo is famous for its many powerful kicks. Experts in taekwondo can break a plank of wood with their kicks or punches.

To do taekwondo successfully, students must be very strong. They must also be able to balance well on one leg so they can complete high, powerful kicks. Taekwondo teachers help their students to become skilled fighters.

But the sport is about more than physical strength. Those who study taekwondo learn how to make their minds peaceful. They also learn to be self-disciplined and courteous.

Colored belts are worn with the taekwondo uniform. Beginners wear white belts. To earn the next belt, students must show they have mastered their current level's techniques. The most experienced students are awarded a black belt.

A KOREAN PROVERB

Sijag-i ban-ida.
시작이 반이다.
"Starting is half the task."

Meaning: Once we begin, we are well on our way to completion.

Kite Flying
Yeon-nal-li-gi 연날리기

Kite battles were popular with Korean men long ago. To prepare the kites for a battle, their strings were coated with ground-up glass. After launching their kites high in the sky, men skillfully made their shield kites swerve and dive, trying to cut the other kites' strings. The battle continued until only one kite was left. Its flyer was the winner.

Today, during the Lunar New Year holiday, Korean families often visit relatives who live in the country. Family members enjoy flying kites (**yeonnalligi**) together. They compete to see who can fly their kite the highest. At the end of the New Year's festivities, some write their name and birthday on their kite, along with a phrase like "Bad luck be gone, good luck stay." Then they let their kite fly away, hoping to have good luck in the coming year.

Make a Simple Korean Shield Kite

Korean shield kites are considered the fastest and toughest fighter kites in the world. Why? They are sturdy, quick and agile, making them great kites for battles. Shaped in a two by three proportion with a hole in the center, shield kites were traditionally made from strong but thin mulberry paper. Shield kites were always decorated with large, bright designs so they could be spotted from a long distance.

It's not easy to make a Korean shield kite, but the kite book listed in the Resources (page 63) gives excellent, detailed directions. You can also make the shield kite shown below quite easily. It's fun to run while this kite flies behind you.

You will need:

- One 8½ by 11" (21cm by 28cm) sheet of paper
- Clear tape
- Strong scissors
- Cup or template to trace a 3" (8cm) circle
- Five 12" (30.5cm) bamboo skewers or sticks
- Three 2' (61cm) pieces of colorful yarn
- Two 30" (76cm) lengths of colorful crepe paper

To make it:

1. The first step is to cut a 3" (8cm) circle out of the center of your paper. To make it easy, fold the paper into quarters. At the corner where the folds meet, use a cup to trace a line marking a quarter circle. Cut on that line, then open the paper to reveal your centered hole.

2. Draw a bright, colorful design on one side of the paper. (This is the side that will face you, as you fly your kite.)

3. Place a bamboo stick across the top of the plain side (the back side) of the paper. Roll the paper around the bamboo stick, to secure it along the top edge of your kite, then tape it in place.

4. Place a small piece of tape on each top corner of the kite, just below each end of the stick. Poke a hole through these 2 tape-reinforced spots.

5. Lay out the other 4 bamboo sticks, as shown: one on each side, and an X in the middle. Trim the sticks so they just reach the edges of the paper. Then tape these sticks in place.

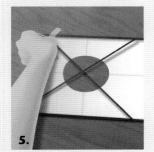

6. Tape crepe paper tails to the bottom corners of your kite.

7. To make a flying bridle, thread a piece of yarn through each of the 2 small holes. Wrap the end of the yarn around the bamboo stick and tie it firmly. Tie the third piece of yarn to the center of the kite, where the sticks cross.

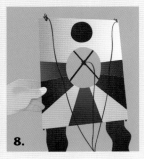

8. Now, gather the 3 lengths of yarn together below your decorated side, and tie them together in a knot about 20" (51cm) down. Tie the yarn again at its very end, to form a loop which you can hold as a flying handle. Fly!

Korean Hacky Sack
Je-gi 제기

What's an early version of the widely-played game hacky-sack? It's **jegi**, a game that began in Korea more than 2,000 years ago. People used to make jegis using a Korean coin that had a hole in the middle. Coins with holes no longer exist in Korea but metal washers work just as well.

Koreans keep **jegis** in the air mainly using the "Nobleman's kick" which means you lift your leg inward, like you are sitting cross-legged, and bat the jegi with the inside of your foot. The kick got its name because Korean noblemen always sat in cross-legged fashion.

Make a Jegi

You will need:

- One metal washer, about 1½" (4cm) across
- 40 pieces of medium yarn, cut into 10" (25cm) lengths

To make it:

1. Fold a yarn piece in half. Put yarn through center of washer.

2. Loop the yarn though itself as shown.

3. Tighten yarn onto washer. Repeat until washer is full of yarn. You're ready to play!

Now try playing Korea's version of hacky-sack. The goal is to keep a jegi in the air as long as you can with your feet. No hands allowed! When you first start, it might be hard. Keep trying! Your score is the number of times you bat the jegi in the air.

You can also play jegi with partners. Begin by gently tossing the jegi to a partner. Tap it back and forth among all players until someone lets it fall. That person is out until the next round. The winner is the one who never let the jegi drop. Pass the jegi well or you will be eliminated!

Korean Balance & Wrestling Game
Dak-ssa-um 닭싸움

Dakssaum is a Korean balancing and wrestling game. Kids often call it "chicken fighting." Traditionally two boys played dakssaum while crowds cheered, but there's nothing to stop girls from being champions at dakssaum, too.

To play:

The game is always played on a grassy spot or a gym mat. Kids are matched to others of similar size.

To begin, each child stands on one leg and bends his other leg in front. He holds onto the foot of his bent leg with his opposite hand. At a signal, the two children begin bumping against each other. They bump into one another until one falls. The child left standing is the winner, who may now face a new opponent.

Playing Korean Jacks
Gong-gi 공기

Gonggi is a popular Korean children's game that's similar to jacks, except there is no ball. You can play it alone or with friends. In times past, Korean children played gonggi using small pebbles. Today, kids buy colorful plastic tokens instead of using pebbles.

To play:

1. Scatter five **gonggi** stones on the ground.
2. Using just one hand, pick up one stone and toss it gently in the air.
3. Before it falls, scoop up a stone from the ground.
4. Catch the falling stone before it hits the ground.
5. Pick all stones up in this same way.

Once you become good at basic gonggi, try these more challenging ways to play.

Advanced Level:

1. Scatter five gonggi stones on the ground. After tossing one in the air, pick up two stones from the ground.
2. During the next round, pick up three stones at one time. Next, try four stones at one time.

Expert Level:

1. Finally, toss a handful of stones lightly in the air.
2. Flip your hand over.
3. Catch as many stones as you can on the back of your hand.
4. Then toss the stones off the back of your hand, catching them in the palm of your hand.
5. The number of stones you catch is the number of points you earn.

Language Lessons

Can You Say It in Korean?

Korea's alphabet is called **hangeul**. It is considered one of the most well designed alphabets in the world. Each character's shape is based on the shape of a person's mouth, throat and tongue when they say the sound!

The hangeul alphabet was invented around 1443 during the reign of the great King Sejong. Before that time, Koreans wrote with complicated Chinese characters. That meant only the rich people, who had lots of time to study, were able to read and write. King Sejong wanted a reading and writing system that everyone could learn, even busy working people, so he created hangeul.

King Sejong would be pleased...almost everyone can read and write in South Korea today.

Now try saying something in Korean!

English	Pronunciation	Hangeul
yes	ne	네
no	aniyo	아니요
hello, how are you?	an-nyeong haseyo	안녕하세요
thank you	gamsa hamnida	감사합니다
mother	eo-meoni	어머니
father	a-beoji	아버지
one	hana	하나
two	dul	둘
three	set	셋
four	net	넷
five	daseot	다섯

Calligraphy
Seo-ye 서예

The word *calligraphy* means "beautiful writing." But Korean calligraphy is far more than just good handwriting. For many hundreds of years, people have admired a carefully crafted calligraphy scroll...just the way they might admire a fine painting.

All Korean children learn calligraphy in school. They practice by carefully copying well-known proverbs like this one:

Ga-hwa-man-sa-seong
가 화 만 사 성
"To succeed in society, we need a happy family first."

Korean Calligraphy Proverb

Try using calligraphy to copy your favorite Korean proverb. Look through this book to choose one.

You will need:
- Black ink or black tempera paint (the paint is easier to clean up than ink)
- Pointed brush with 1" (2.5cm) bristles (a firmer brush is better for beginners)
- Practice paper
- A 4" x 17" (10cm x 44cm) sheet of good quality paper

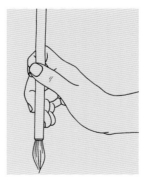

To make it:
1. Practice your strokes on paper scraps before beginning.
2. Hold your paintbrush gently in an upright position, supporting the brush; follow the diagrams at right.
3. Dip the brush tip into ink. Change the pressure on your brush to get different thicknesses for your lines.
4. Hang your best work up, since it is a special piece of art!

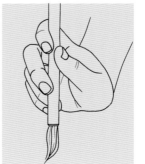

In old times, Korean men would have a special low desk, where they kept the "Scholar's Four Friends." The "Scholar's Four Friends" is a name for the tools you use for calligraphy: a brush, paper, an ink stick and an ink stone. You rub the ink stick against the ink stone with water, to make your own ink.

A KOREAN PROVERB

Aneun gil-do mureo gara.
아는 길도 물어 가라.
"Even if you know the way, ask one more time."

Meaning: It would be wise to make sure before you take action.

Fan dancers performed for the royal court, dressed in silky **hanboks**. The dance was serene and graceful to honor their king.

Music and Dance

Toes Tap and Fans Fly!

Koreans have always enjoyed music, especially singing and drumming. Long ago, Korean royalty and the wealthy people listened to the slow and serious melodies of the style called "court music." And common people liked the lively rhythms of the style called "folk music."

Today, Koreans like many styles of music and dance. They are very fond of karaoke. But traditional Korean music is as treasured today as it has been for centuries.

In days past, court musicians played horns, flutes, harps and stringed instruments to entertain the royalty during banquets and religious ceremonies. Korea's best-known traditional instrument is the 12-stringed **gayageum**.

Country people traditionally played folk music during the spring season hoping for good crops, or during the fall in thanks for a good harvest. Farmer bands used drums, gongs and flutes to play melodies that were simple, but the strong rhythms and energy made their music unforgettable.

Want to experience Korean music or dance? It's never been easier! Type "Korean drumming," "Korean fan dance" or "gayageum" into a computer search engine, to find some of the fine recordings posted on the internet. While listening to a recording of Korean drumming, tap out the rhythm using your Korean drum. Notice how the rhythm changes.

Make a Buk Drum

You will need:

- An empty round oatmeal carton with lid
- Colored construction paper
- Tape, safety scissors, glue stick and a pencil

To make it:

1. Trace the end of the oatmeal carton onto the construction paper twice. Cut out both circles and glue them to the ends of the carton.

2. Wrap the carton in colored construction paper. Cut the paper to fit, then tape it in place.

3. To make your drum look more authentic, decorate the paper before putting it on the drum. You can study the illustrations in this book for some decorating ideas.

The dance called **samulnori** is based on the farmer's dance, one of Korea's oldest folk dances. Lively dancers wear hats decorated with long, colorful ribbons attached on top. Gongs and round drums called **buk** keep the beat as dancers play double-headed hourglass-shaped **janggu** drums. They twirl, spin and flick their heads, making the ribbons float through the air.

Singing Time

Koreans Love to Sing!

Koreans love to sing! In days past, Koreans sang while working in the fields to help pass the time. "Arirang" is Korea's favorite and most powerful folk song.

What does "arirang" mean? There's no exact English translation, but it has a message of "accepting pain as a part of life." Koreans have sung the verses of "Arirang" to overcome all kinds of hardships. With a history of wars and separations, it is not surprising that Koreans feel a sense of closeness when they sing "Arirang" together.

Arirang 아리랑

A-ri-rang, a-ri-rang, a-ra-ri - yo
아 리 랑 -, 아 리 랑 -, 아 라 - 리 - 요
A-ri-rang, a-ri-rang, a-ra-ri - yo

A-ri-rang go - gae-ro neomeo ganda.
아 리 랑 - 고 - 개 - 로 - 넘 어 간 다.
O-ver the - A - ri - rang hill you must go.

Na-reul beori-go ga sineun nim - eun,
나 를 버 리 고 가 시 는 님 - 은,
How I wish you would not go - a - way,

Simni - do - mot - ga - seo - balbyeong nanda.
십 리 - 도 못 - 가 - 서 - 발 병 난 다.
It is such a lo-ng wa-lk and I want you to stay.

30

Friendship Facts

- Koreans greatly value their friendships. They give gifts as a sign of friendship.
- Losing one's temper is considered very bad manners.
- Koreans often greet anyone older than themselves with a small bow.

Nun = eyes

Ko = nose

Gwi = ears

Meori = head

Eokkae = shoulders

Bal = feet

Mureup = knees

Head, Shoulders, Knees and Feet
Meori, Eokkae, Mureup, Bal 머리 어깨 무릎 발

This popular action song can easily be sung in Korean. But take note! The tune is the same but the Korean words are a bit different from the song you might be used to.

Meo-ri, eo-kkae, mureup, bal, mureup, bal
머리 어깨 무릎 발 무릎 발
Head, shoulders, knees, feet, knees, feet

Meo-ri, eo-kkae, mureup, bal, mureup, bal
머리 어깨 무릎 발 무릎 발
Head, shoulders, knees, feet, knees, feet

Meori, eokkae, bal -, mureup, bal
머리 어깨 발 - 무릎 발
Head, shoulders, feet, knees, feet

Meo - ri, eokkae, mureup, nun, ko -, gwi!
머 리 어깨 무릎 눈 코 - 귀!
Head, shoulders, knees, eyes, nose, ears!

32

A Korean Lullaby
Ja-jang-ga 자장가

Parents around the world sing to their little ones to help them get to sleep. This is Korea's most well-known lullaby. It was written by Kim Dae-hyun 김 대 현 .

Uri agi, chak-han a - gi sorok sorok jamdeul-la
우 리 아 기, 착 한 아 - 기 소 록 소 록 잠 들 라
My baby, good ba - by, sleep a sound sleep,

Haneul nara agi byeo - ldo eomma pum-e jamdeunda
하 늘 나 라 아 기 별 - 도 엄 마 품 에 잠 든 다
Baby stars in the - sky, fall asleep nestled in mother's breast,

Dung-dung a gi jamja - geo - ra ye-bbeun a gi ja - jang.
둥 둥 아 기 잠 자 거 - 라 예 쁜 아 기 자 - 장.
My adorable baby, please sleep well, my pretty baby, hushabye.

Korean Arts and Crafts

Bold and Beautiful

From paintings to sculptures to careful building designs, Korean art often has the theme of "being in harmony with nature."

   Although Japanese, Chinese and Korean artwork share some things in common, Korean art is especially known for...

• Amazing pottery, especially the elegantly simple, jade-green pottery called **celadon**.

• Special ways of using paper.

• Some of the world's finest sculptures of Buddha.

• Calligraphy. It's more than writing in Korea: it is a form of art.

• Masks. Some Korean masks look silly. Others are grotesque or beautiful. Over time, the remarkable masks from Korea have been used in wars, in ceremonies, to drive away evil spirits...and today, even as key chains!

• Clothes and wall hangings decorated with colorful, finely detailed embroidery.

34

Make a Korean Paper Box

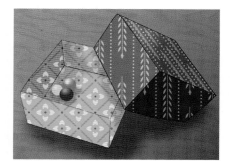

Koreans have been using paper since at least the fourth century. Long ago, Koreans used paper for windows and doors, for building cabinets and desks, and to make many household items like combs, bowls and jars. Some of these items were varnished to make them shiny, strong and waterproof.

This little folded box can hold keepsakes or be filled with a small but special gift.

You will need:

- 2 square sheets of paper, at least 6" x 6" (15cm x 15cm) in size. Sturdy wrapping paper works best.

To make it:

1. Begin with the paper colored side down. Fold the first sheet in half to make a triangle. Open sheet. Repeat fold on the other diagonal.

2. Fold one corner in to the center. Open sheet. Repeat with all corners.

3. Fold the corner to meet its closest fold. Open sheet. Repeat with all corners.

4. Fold the corner to meet the fold line across the center fold. Open sheet. Repeat with all corners. Now all the fold lines are in place!

5. To begin to shape the box, first fold the top and bottom corners in to meet at the center. Now fold the top and bottom edges in to meet at the center. Then unfold the edges back halfway, so they form 2 sides standing up at right angles from the bottom. The first 2 sides of your box are complete!

6. Now you will fold the 3rd side. Push a finger in at each of the two spots marked on the diagram, and fold the point in to reach the center of the box's bottom.

7. You will need to pinch and adjust as you do this folding, to make the box's new side and corners sharp and symmetrical.

8. Repeat Steps 6 and 7 on the final corner. This creates the 4th side of your box.

9. Using the other square of paper, repeat all steps to create the box bottom. Ease the triangle folds slightly in Step 6 to make the boxes fit well together.

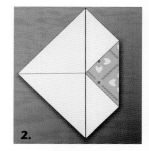

2.

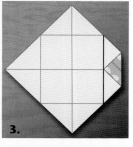

3.

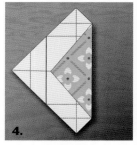

4.

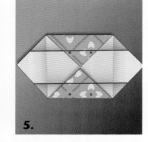

5.

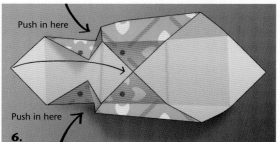

Push in here

Push in here

6.

7.

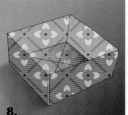

8.

The Many Masks of Korea

Long ago, Korean mask dances were a part of religious ceremonies. Later, mask dances were performed outdoors by farmers and common people, giving them a break from their hard work. They acted out mask dances to poke fun at powerful people like government officials or scholars. During Korean mask dance dramas, the audience often joins in, clapping and laughing and even dancing with the performers.

Korean masks are usually made from wood, gourds or paper mache. Their colors and details make it easy to recognize the different characters of a mask dance. A few of the most familiar are:

- **Nobleman Mask:** This has a long black beard, and a trick. When the actor holds his head up, the mask looks cheerful. When he looks down, the mask looks mean.

- **Scholar Mask:** In mask dramas, the Scholar thought he was better than other people. Though he is supposed to be studying, he wastes much time.

- **Old Granny:** She has a small, wrinkled face that shows she has had a hard life. In mask dramas, Granny often gossips about what others are doing.

Make a Paper-mache Mask

You will need:
- Aluminum foil
- Tape
- Tempera paint
- Elastic strap
- Newspaper
- Glue
- Paintbrush

To make it:

1. To make a cast of your face, cut a long piece of aluminum foil. Fold it over 3 or 4 times so that it is slightly larger than your face.

2. Have a friend press the foil gently into all parts of your face.

3. Remove carefully. Roll the foil edges to make a small rim.

4. Carefully fill your face mold with crumpled newspaper. Tape the rolled edge to hold it in place.

5. Make a paste from equal parts water and glue.

6. Cut or tear strips of newspaper and dip them into the glue mixture. Gently place wet strips over the face mold until its entire surface is covered. Let it dry overnight.

7. Repeat Step 6 two more times, for a thicker mask. Use twisted newspaper to add details like horns, ears, or a nose. When completely dry, remove the newspaper stuffing. Ask a grown up to help you cut eyeholes.

8. Add a final layer of paper strips, as in Step 6, if you want to make the mask surface smoother.

9. When it is dry, paint your mask. Then add an elastic strap, "hair," "beard," or other decorations.

Hanboks for the Holidays

Korea's traditional clothing is called the hanbok. Before the arrival of Western-style clothing 100 years ago, hanboks were what people wore every day in Korea. Wealthy Koreans always wore colorful hanboks but everyone else usually wore white hanboks.

Today almost all Koreans wear Western-style clothing, but people still wear vibrant colored hanboks during holidays and for special occasions.

Jeogori 저고리
A loose-fitting top that covers the arms and upper body. You can see its white and green collar peeking out at the man's and the boy's neck.

Durumagi 두루마기
A topcoat worn to keep warm. The man is wearing a brown one.

Magoja 마고자
A short jacket worn over the **jeogori**. The boy is wearing a blue one.

Baji 바지
Wide, baggy comfortable pants that are tied at the ankles and waist.

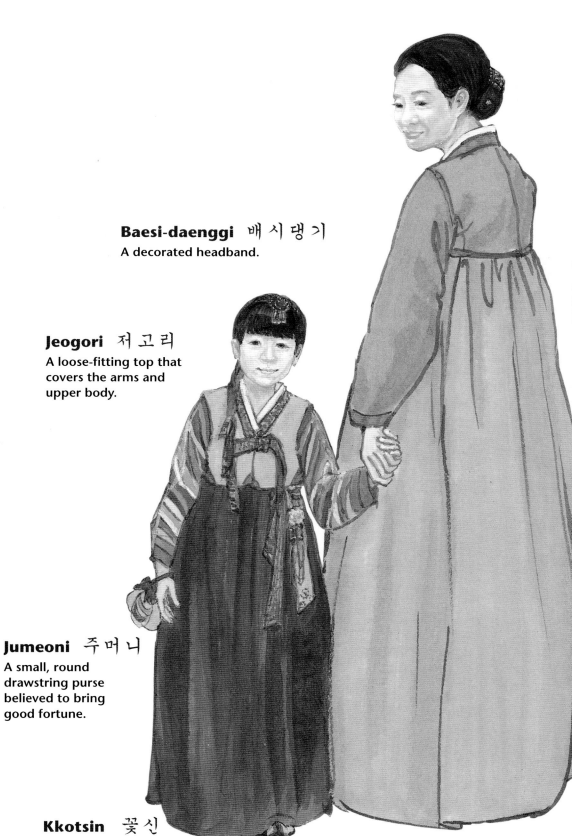

Baesi-daenggi 배시댕기
A decorated headband.

Jeogori 저고리
A loose-fitting top that covers the arms and upper body.

Jumeoni 주머니
A small, round drawstring purse believed to bring good fortune.

Kkotsin 꽃신
Embroidered silk shoes.

Chima 치마
A wide, wrap-around skirt that is tied high, just under the arms.

Norigae
노리개
A charm that hangs from the jacket. Thought to bring good luck, **norigae** are often handed down from mothers to their daughters.

Home Sweet Home

Sarangbang 사랑방
In old times men and older boys always had separate rooms from the women and girls. The **sarangbang** or men's room, near the entrance gate, was a home's receiving room. Here wealthy Korean men would have a low desk, an inkstone and brushes for calligraphy, rolled paper scrolls, and books.

Ondol 온돌
Koreans heated their homes through the floor with a system called **ondol**. The heat of the kitchen fire was sent through the house with a network of stone ducts and flues. During warm weather, the flues were closed and the warm air was sent out chimneys instead.

Anbang 안방
The women's room was near the kitchen in the protected back part of the house. In old days, women cooked, heated water and kept the fire going. In their room women kept a dowry box filled with gifts for the family of future husbands, chests with clothes and blankets, and sewing supplies. All children slept in this room with their mothers, girls until they married and boys until they started school.

Traditionally, Korean homes were one story. Homes of the wealthy had tile roofs but most homes had thatched roofs. There was usually a wall surrounding each house so that even if neighboring homes were nearby, a small interior courtyard gave a family some privacy.

Bu-eok 부엌
The only completely separate room of the house, the kitchen had cooking tools, a cooking hearth, and shelves filled with bowls, plates, and baskets.

Jangdokdae 장독대
This was the special place to store jars of **kimchi**, soy sauce, red pepper paste and pickled vegetables.

Sinbal 신발
Sinbal (shoes) were always removed before entering a home. Since people sat on the floor, floors were kept spotlessly clean.

Maru 마루
The **maru** was a covered veranda that served as a dining room, living room, playroom, and study. This was a favorite spot to gather. It had a small amount of furniture, always low and moveable. People sat on cushions on the clean floor. During summertime, the roof provided shade and the open walls allowed a welcome breeze. During cooler weather, screen panels were put up to keep out cold and dampness.

Where do most Koreans live today? In apartments! Traditional Korean houses are still found in the countryside but with Korea's nearly 50 million people, most open flat land is needed for farming. Well-designed high-rise apartments are a good way to fit many homes into a small space. Korean apartments are modern and efficient but it's interesting to notice how their layouts are similar to Korean homes of the past.

Hyeon-gwan-mun 현관문

The front door has taken the place of the entrance gate found in traditional Korean homes. It leads into the living area, or maru, Koreans always take off their shoes when indoors. Guests are usually offered slippers. It keeps floors cleaner, which is especially important because people continue to sit on the floor. Shoes are kept by the front door.

Beranda 베란다

Apartments often have front and back verandas or balconies which allow in fresh cooling breezes. The front balcony is often set up nicely with chairs and tables for enjoying the breezes while the back veranda, located near the kitchen, is used for more practical matters like washing clothes and storage.

Try it!

Take off your shoes every time you come inside for a week. Was this hard to do? Did your house stay cleaner?

Anbang 안방

Today, married couples sleep together in the **anbang**, the bedroom. Older Koreans continue to sleep on mats, which are folded away in the day to give room for other activities, but younger Koreans most often choose to sleep in Western-style beds.

Bang 방

Extra bedrooms are used by children or by guests. Korean technology is cutting edge, and today most Koreans have computers, which are usually placed in a **bang**.

Bu-eok 부엌

Most cooking is done on a stovetop, so many kitchens do not have an oven. If they do it is used very little. Many families have dishwashers but some older Koreans prefer to wash dishes by hand.

Maru 마루

The living room is located in the center of the apartment. Koreans sit on the floor when extra people are visiting but almost all Korean living rooms have couches. Most Koreans eat their meals on chairs at a dining table but almost all families also have a very large, low table, which serves as a dining table when guests are visiting.

Ondol 온돌

Korean apartments are heated with an **ondol** heating system, which is basically hot water that runs through pipes in the floor. This heating system makes it really cozy to sit on the floor.

Korean Food Is Delicious

Scrumptious and Spicy!

Korean foods are full of flavor and some dishes are quite spicy! This isn't surprising since Koreans use red pepper, green onion, soy sauce, bean paste, garlic, ginger, sesame and mustard to flavor their foods. Rice and kimchi are served with every meal. Most Korean meals also include soup, a main dish that is a mixture of meat or seafood, noodles with vegetables, and a variety of flavorful side dishes.

Nowadays, like most people, Koreans also eat many foods from other places. Pizza is very popular among the younger generation, but Koreans still enjoy the flavors of traditional Korean cuisine!

A side dish that is served with every meal, **kimchi** 김치 best represents Korean food. It tastes spicy and sour at the same time, and is made of cabbage, cucumber or radish that is pickled in a salty brine of green onion, ginger, garlic and chili pepper powder.

Barbecued Beef Recipe
Bul-go-gi 불고기

Bulgogi is a favorite dish in Korea. Tasty barbecued bulgogi is served with kimchi and white rice, and is sometimes wrapped together in a lettuce leaf. Bulgogi can be made of any type of meat, but beef and pork are most popular.

This recipe calls for a wok or a skillet, but the flavors will be even better if the meat is cooked on a grill, which is the traditional way in Korea.

Equipment you will need:
Large mixing bowl, mixing spoon, wok or large skillet, knife, measuring cup and spoon.

Ingredients:
1 pound lean boneless sirloin or round steak
4 Tablespoons sesame oil
6 whole green onions, finely chopped
4 teaspoons sugar or to taste
4 teaspoons toasted sesame seeds

½ cup soy sauce
½ teaspoon black pepper
4 cloves garlic, minced
4 Tablespoons vegetable oil

To make it:
1. Have the butcher or meat department cut the meat ⅙" thick. Korean markets often sell the meat precut.

2. Put soy sauce, sesame oil, pepper, green onions and garlic in a bowl. Mix well. Add the meat, coating it thoroughly. Cover and let soak at room temperature for 2 hours, or in the refrigerator overnight. Mix often to keep the meat coated. Add the sugar and let it soak for 30 minutes at room temperature.

3. Heat the vegetable oil in a wok or skillet over high heat. Drain the beef and place in the wok. Stir constantly until it is cooked through, about 3 minutes. Cut into strips 2" (5cm) long. Place on serving platter. Sprinkle with sesame seeds.

Serves 4

Be safe!
Hold your knife firmly and keep your fingers away from the blade. Before you begin cooking, be sure to ask a grown up for permission and for help, especially with knives and the stove.

How to Use Chopsticks
Jeot-ga-rak 젓가락

Koreans use metal spoons when they eat soup or stew but they use chopsticks to eat most foods.

Try It!

Use chopsticks to eat a meal. It isn't all that hard; just follow these simple steps:

1. Place the upper part of one chopstick between your thumb and forefinger. Hold the lower half of that stick firmly against your ring finger. This chopstick does not move.

2. Hold the other chopstick like you hold a pencil.

3. Move this chopstick by pressing up with your thumb. Move the top chopstick up and down to pick up food from your plate.

Vegetable, Rice, and Barbecued Meat Roll
Kim-bap 김밥

Korean kids love **kimbap**. It's a favorite because it is easily adapted to suit everybody's taste. The main idea is to slice all ingredients finely and roll them tightly into seaweed rolls. Kimbap is often rolled with barbecued beef (though chicken, hotdog, ham or tuna are also tasty) along with **kimchi**, fried egg, or pickled radishes or other vegetables. Korean markets sell many fine side dishes that are great in kimbap. (See Resources on page 63.)

Ingredients:

4 cups cooked rice
½ teaspoon soy sauce
2 eggs, beaten
4 large sheets of dried seaweed
1 carrot, cut into thin strips
Pickled radishes or other vegetables,
   or **kimchi**

½ teaspoon rice vinegar
1 teaspoon sesame oil
Bulgogi (recipe on page 45) or barbecued meat of
   your choice
1 Tablespoon sesame seeds, toasted

To make it:

1. Cool the rice. Mix it with the vinegar, soy sauce and sesame oil.

2. Fry the egg as if it were a pancake and cut it into strips.

3. Cut the meat into thin strips.

4. Follow the directions below to roll your kimbap!

   Serves 4

Rolling kimbap:

1. Place a seaweed sheet on a bamboo rolling mat. Spread rice over two thirds of the sheet.

2. Lay carrots, meat, egg, pickled radish or other ingredients on the rice. Sprinkle with sesame seeds.

3. Place a few pieces of cooked rice on the edge of the seaweed where there is no rice. Carefully fold the rice-filled end onto itself. Roll tightly.

4. When you reach the end, use the bamboo mat to help press and seal the edge of the seaweed sheet against the roll. The bits of rice will act as "glue."

5. Have a grown up use a sharp knife to cut the roll into 12 pieces. To keep the knife from sticking, wipe it off with a wet cloth after each slice. Arrange your kimbap on a plate with cut side up.

 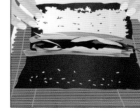

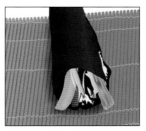 

The Keys to Success

Education Rules!

Education is very important to Koreans today. Korean children are expected to study hard. Mothers often help their children with studies. In Korea, people believe that a university education is the key to success...and to get into a university, kids must first pass an important test called the entrance exam. At the end of the school day, many children go to "cram school" to prepare for it. It is hard to be accepted into Korean universities, so the pressure is on for Korean kids, even very young ones, to get ready for entrance exams!

Showing Respect

Koreans believe it is very important to show each other respect whenever possible. Here are just a few of the ways they show respect to one another:

Parents try to treat their children with kindness and respect. Parents feel this also shows respect to their ancestors.

Korean children feel it is their duty to obey their parents. Children work hard in school to show their parents respect.

Children never call an adult by their first name. Rather, they call them "elder man" (**ajeossi**, 아저씨) or "elder woman" (**ajumeoni**, 아주머니) as a sign of respect.

Children are expected to clean their classrooms each day to show they value their education.

Respect for elders is especially important. Koreans offer elders their seat on a bus, never interrupt when an elder is speaking, and bow (**jeol**, 절) to elders during special occasions like New Year's Day.

Two Foolish Green Frogs

Have you ever wondered why frogs croak on muddy riverbanks? This story is the Korean explanation. The Korean word for frog *is gae-guri, and that's also the sound it makes: "gae-gul, gae-gul." Korean children who don't obey their parents are called "cheong gae-guri" or "green frogs." Read the story to understand why!*

Long ago two young frogs lived with their mother by a lily pond. Sons are usually a blessing but this pair caused their mother a lot of worry. You see, they never did as they were told. They did exactly the opposite of what their mother wanted, just to be difficult.

One day when they were very young, Mother Frog called, "Sons, come for breakfast!"

Did the little green frogs listen to their mother? No, of course not! The brothers swam into the pond instead and dove off lily pads. Mother called, "Sons, you are too young to swim so far! Please come ashore and we'll have breakfast." But the frogs laughed and swam on and on.

Finally, Mother shouted, "Fine, skip breakfast! It leaves more for me." Quick as a wink, the brothers swam to shore and gobbled their breakfast.

In the hot afternoon, Mother settled down for a nap and told the little frogs, "Time to be quiet." But did the young frogs listen to their mother? No, of course not! The frogs naughtily yelled out some practice croaks—backward: "Gul-gae! GUL-GAE!"

Mother sighed. She explained, "You have it backward. 'Gae-gul! Gae-gul!' is the way we croak." The young frogs giggled and kept on croaking backward: "Gul-gae! Gul-gae!"

Another day Mother said, "My sons, there are hungry foxes in the hills, so please play in the valley today."

But did the young frogs listen to their mother? No, of course not! They hopped straight to the hills and chased grasshoppers. The frogs were so busy playing that they didn't notice a pair of foxes slinking toward them.

"Look out!" yelled Mother, coming up the hill to find her sons. "Foxes are after you!"

The brothers hopped into the creek, just barely escaping the foxes' hungry teeth. Back at their lily pond, the brothers laughed, "Aren't we tricky to outsmart foxes?"

Mother scolded, "You could have been those foxes' supper!" which just made the little frogs laugh even harder.

Somehow Mother remained hopeful. She thought, "Perhaps my sons will grow wise with age."

This was not to be. Through winter, spring, summer and fall, year after year, the frog brothers did exactly as they pleased, never listening to their poor mother.

One day Mother said, "It's been raining long and hard. The river is too dangerous. Please go up into the hills to catch supper." But did the brothers listen to their mother? No, of course not! They hopped straight into the raging river to hunt for minnows. As her sons swam off, Mother shouted, "Be careful! You'll be pulled downstream."

The brothers chuckled as they swam toward the middle of the rushing river. The frogs were strong swimmers, but the current that day was too powerful. In an instant, the brothers were swirling toward a waterfall. "Help! Help!" they cried.

Mother croaked helplessly as her sons were pulled downstream. She could not bear to watch as her dear sons shot over the waterfall. She sprang along the riverbank to search for them.

Finding them finally, Mother dragged her injured sons from the water and frantically tended their many cuts and scrapes. Luck was with the foolish frogs. After weeks of their mother's tender care, both brothers recovered. But sadly, Mother did not.

Worn down with work and worry, Mother could barely lift her head. When it was clear she would not live long, Mother called her sons to her lily pad. "Sons, all your lives you have disobeyed me. I ask you to obey me just this once. When I die, do NOT bury me in my favorite grassy meadow above our lily pond. Please bury me in the muddy ground beside the river."

Now, Mother frog honestly wanted to be buried in the meadow above her beloved lily pond. But she thought the only way her wish would be fulfilled was if she asked for the opposite.

The sons were heartbroken when their mother died. With deep regret they said, "Why did we always disobey Mother?"

After a long silence, one brother said, "Perhaps we can make it up to her. Let's obey Mother's last request." With that, the brothers respectfully buried their mother in the muddy ground by the river.

That night, fierce rains began. The frog brothers sat mournfully by their mother's grave, croaking to the river, "Gae-gul! Gae-gul! Please don't wash Mother away!"

The rain continued and the river swelled. All night long the worried brothers never left their mother's grave. Other frogs joined their chorus: "Gae-gul! Gae-gul! Please don't wash Mother away!"

And to this day, during rainstorms, green frogs still gather on riverbanks calling, "Gae-gul! Gae-gul! Please don't wash Mother away!"

Family, Fun and Festivities

Koreans have been influenced by many religions and beliefs through the centuries, so Korea celebrates more kinds of holidays than most countries. Independence Day, Children's Day, Buddha's Birthday, the Harvest Moon festival and Christmas are just a few. And Koreans celebrate New Year twice! Once according to the lunar calendar, and once according to the "solar" Gregorian calendar.

Lunar New Year
Seol 설

Lunar New Year is one of the biggest holidays of the Korean year. **Seol** is usually around February 1st, when no moon can be seen. To prepare for New Year, Koreans do a careful housecleaning and they cook lots of wonderful foods, including **tteokguk** 떡국, rice cake soup. (For a recipe, visit www.tuttlepublishing.com.) The cities become quiet and empty during Seol as many Koreans take a holiday from work and visit their relatives who live in the country.

Koreans wake up early on Seol and dress in their best hanboks. Then Koreans prepare for **Charye** 차례, a ceremony to honor and remember family members who have died. An altar table is carefully filled with incense sticks and many food dishes. There are traditions about what foods should be on an altar but people tend to offer food the person liked most when they were alive. They offer every dish in a special way, since Koreans believe that if departed relatives are fed well, they will be strong enough to bless their living family. Everyone bows before the table, to show respect to the relatives who are dead. Koreans often visit family members' graves, honoring them again there.

An important part of the day is when children do a special bow to their elders—a bow so low that their foreheads touch the ground. The elders in turn give money and a bit of advice to the children. After enjoying a wonderful feast together, it is time to play! Families play Korea's traditional games like Korean See-saw and **jegi**, and kite flying is still a favorite activity in the countryside.

First Full Moon of the New Year

Dae-bo-reum 대보름

Daeboreum is the last day of Lunar New Year festivities. It is also the day when Korea's new planting season begins.

During the festivals on this day, people bang loudly on drums and gongs, hoping to drive away the evil spirits of the old year and bring peace, health and good fortune in the coming year.

Then, in the evening, people gather in town squares to enjoy the first full moon of the year.

Children's Day
Eo-rin-i-nal 어린이날

Why do Koreans celebrate **Eorininal**, Children's Day, every May 5th? A children's writer named Pang Chong-hwan invented this holiday in 1923, explaining: "Children are the future of our nation. Let's show respect for children. A child who grows up with ridicule and contempt from others will become someone who disrespects others, while a child who grows up with respect from others will become someone who respects others in turn." So Children's Day is a reminder to Koreans that every child needs love, care and respect.

Children's Day is fun! Schools and most businesses close so families can spend the day together. Some families attend parades or local festivals. Others play games together. Some families visit amusement parks, museums, zoos or movie theaters, and these places offer free admission to kids. Children receive gifts from their parents and even from some stores. And of course, at the end of the day, families enjoy a delicious meal together.

Spring Festival
Dan-o 단오

In days past, **Dano** was a day to celebrate the beginning of spring. Koreans spent the day outdoors playing games, basking in the warmer weather and enjoying the beauty of spring. Dano isn't celebrated much anymore but some of the day's special activities, like riding see-saws and swings, are still enjoyed during other Korean holidays.

The Korean See-saw
Neol-ttwi-gi 널뛰기

In the West, kids sit on either end of a see-saw but in Korea, children stand on see-saws that are close to the ground. When one child lands on a see-saw, the child on the opposite end jumps in the air. If the kids balance well while jumping in a steady rhythm, the pair can bounce each other higher and higher.

Long ago, Korean girls over the age of seven were rarely allowed to leave their family's yard. It is believed girls developed the see-saw game to see what was going on beyond the high walls of their yards. On festival days, some girls and women still dress in their best hanboks and put on a show of skill on the see-saw.

Play Korean See-saw

You will need:

- 3 players
- 2 adults (when first learning)
- A wooden board, 10' (3m) long, 12" (30.5cm) wide by 2" (5cm) thick
- A 50-pound (23kg) bag of grain or birdseed
- A soft, grassy playing area

To play:

1. Center the bag of grain under the middle of the board so the board tips evenly.

2. One child squats in the middle of the board and puts a hand on each side for balance.

3. Two children stand on either end of the board and begin taking turns jumping.

4. When one child lands, the other jumps into the air.

5. If the children use a steady rhythm, they will launch each other higher and higher.

6. If kids are beginners, adults should stand next to each jumper and offer a hand for balance.

Korean Swing
Geu-ne 그네

In the old days, swinging was a favorite exercise for girls. Two girls often stood on the swing at the same time. They would fly through the air and work together to go as high as they could. Since Korean swings were very tall, geune was truly a test of balance and nerves.

Traditionally girls took part in swinging competitions during **Dano** or **Hangawi**. Sometimes swingers used their feet to ring a bell that hung high in the air.

Long ago, Koreans hung swings from a branch of a tall willow or pine tree using long, strong ropes. These days, swings are hung from a frame, which can be as tall as 36 feet (11m)!

60th Birthday Celebration
Hwan-gap 환갑

Try It!

Sing Korea's birthday song! It's pretty simple since "Saeng-il chukha-hamnida" is sung to the same tune as "Happy Birthday to You."

Happy Birthday to You
Saeng-il chukha-hamnida

Saeng-il chukha-hamnida,
생일　　축하합니다,
Happy birthday to you,

Saeng-il chukha-hamnida,
생일　　축하합니다,
Happy birthday to you,

Sarang-haneun _____ -ssi,
사랑하는 _____－씨,
My lovely friend _____,

Saeng-il chukha-hamnida!
생일　　축하합니다!
Happy birthday to you!

Sixty years is a long time. When a Korean person turns 60, friends and family celebrate them as an "honored person" who has lived a full life. There may be feasting, music, singing, poetry…maybe even a magic show!

A special time is set aside to honor the 60-year-old and his or her spouse. While traditional Korean music is played, the family members, oldest to youngest, bow to the person who's being honored. Then friends pay their respects in the same way.

No **Hwangap** would be complete without a photograph of the 60-year-old surrounded by his or her children and grandchildren.

Babies are older in Korea than you might expect! That's because the day a baby is born, he or she is considered to be one year old. Also, Koreans add one year to everyone's age on New Year's Day rather than on birthdays, so people in Korea are considered 1 or 2 years older than they would be in Western nations.

A Baby's 100th Day Celebration
Baeg-il 백일

Families host a big celebration on their baby's 100th day of life. Friends and family come to admire and bring gifts to the baby, and the family gives 100 steamed rice cakes to 100 people, in the hope that their child will have a long life.

A Child's First Birthday
Dol 돌

Many Korean families give a special party on their child's first birthday. During **Dol**, the birthday child is placed on cushions at a low table so that everyone can see and admire him or her. The baby is beautifully dressed in a colorful hanbok. His or her outfit includes a long belt to ensure a long life, and there is a silk pouch to bring good luck.

A ceremony is held to predict the birthday child's future. Certain items are put out on a table, and everyone watches to see the first thing the baby grabs. For example, if she grabs a pencil or book, it means she will be a scholar. Rice means the child will be rich. Thread means the child will have a long life.

The guests give the baby gifts. There is a cake with candles, the singing of "Happy Birthday"—the Korean version, that is—and wishes to the baby for a long and happy life.

The Harvest Moon Festival
Han-ga-wi 한가위

Hangawi (한가위), also called **Chuseok** (추석), is Korea's harvest festival. It is celebrated in either September or October during the eighth full moon of the year. In days past, Koreans spent Hangawi relaxing because the crops were harvested and farm work was done for the year. These days, airports, trains and roads are jammed as Koreans return to their hometowns to visit family members, visit relatives' graves and celebrate the fall harvest.

Many Koreans begin Hangawi by visiting the graves of dead family members. After pulling weeds and tidying up their ancestors' graves, Koreans place food there from the latest harvest. Then they bow low, offering thanks to their ancestors for their good fortune. Some families also do a bowing ceremony at home. Koreans spend the rest of the holiday having fun together. Families enjoy a wonderful meal and the tasty dessert called **songpyeon**.

Sweet Filled Rice Cakes
Song-pyeon 송편

If you visited a Korean family a few days before **Hangawi**, you would likely find people of all ages shaping rice dough into half-moon-shaped **songpyeon**. Children love their chewy skin and surprising semi-sweet fillings. You can easily make this dessert with just a small amount of adult help. There are many kinds of fillings but this one is a classic.

Equipment you will need:

- 2 bowls
- vegetable steamer
- tongs
- muslin cloth

Ingredients:

1½ cups rice flour (see Resources)
Pinch of salt
¼ cup hot water
3 Tablespoons roasted sesame seeds
2 Tablespoons honey or corn syrup or rice syrup (see Resources)
½ Tablespoon sesame oil
Extra honey for dipping

To make it:

1. Combine the rice flour with the salt. Add the hot water, a teaspoon at a time, to the flour mixture, stirring constantly. Once all the water has been added, knead the dough until its texture is smooth. Cover the dough with a clean, damp cloth.

2. Mix the sesame seeds and honey together to form a paste. Set aside.

3. Roll a walnut-sized piece of dough into a ball. Make a pocket in the dough ball with your fingers. Fill it with ½ teaspoon of the sesame-honey paste. Close the top of the ball and gently mold into a half-moon shape, to create each rice cake.

4. Place the muslin cloth in the vegetable steamer then set a single layer of the rice cakes into the steamer. Steam the cakes for 15 minutes. Place the cakes and the sesame oil into a small bowl, and toss to coat. Serve warm, with honey for dipping.

Eating Etiquette

Each culture has rules for what is considered polite while eating. Here are some of Korea's key table manners:

Do not use your fingers to tear food.

The eldest person begins eating first.

Do not blow your nose during meals.

Everyone must stay at the table until the elder is finished.

Chopsticks should not be left in rice or soup bowls.

Acknowledgments

As a non-Korean, it would have been impossible for me to write this book without the help and insights of many. Thank you Chris Winston, Denise Park, Young Seo Lee, Chong Byun, Chris LaCava, Jeong Spztzla, Erin Dealey, Steve Hall, Malcolm Dick, Dr. Euyoungso Park, Michelle Worley, Jeong Shin, Dr. Soohee Kim, Kyongsook Kim, Soomgyul Saebul, and all the families of Sacramento's Friends of Korea School! A giant thank you Jung Lee for patiently answering my endless questions. Many kudos to my fine editor, Sandra Korinchak; you made this book shine. Thanks to Tan Cheng Har and the Tuttle graphics and layout staff for all your hard work. Many thanks to Soonsoonam Barg. Your lovely illustrations bring the Korean culture to life. And finally, thanks to Sarah and Jacob for helping me with this book and to my entire family for your continual support. I hope you enjoyed this project as much as I did!

Resources

Helpful Internet Sites

http://www.korea.net Offers Korean news, maps, travel tips, historical and cultural information.

http://www.visitkorea.or.kr/intro.html Great site for those planning a trip to Korea.

http://www.askasia.org Reliable information about Asia designed for students and teachers.

http://goldsea.com A list of notable Asian Americans.

http://www.inkas.or.kr/eng/index.asp Helpful website for Korean adoptees and their families.

http://www.kaanet.com Helpful website for Korean adoptees and their families.

http://www.koreanfeast.com/korean_markets_in_the_us.htm A list of U.S. Korean markets.

http://www.kaanet.com/asian_links/ Links to many websites, including sources for purchasing Korean items.

http://www.asiaforkids.com An online catalogue offering language and culture books, videos, CD-ROMS, crafts, games, dolls and music.

Recommended Reading

Yunmi and Halmoni's Trip by Sook Nyul Choi, illustrated by Karen Dugan (Houghton Mifflin, 1997). Ages 4 & up.

Bee-Bim Bop by Linda Sue Park, illustrated by Bo Baek Lee (Clarion, 2005). Ages 2–6.

The Firekeeper's Son by Linda Sue Park, illustrated by Julia Downing (Clarion, 2004). Ages 4–8.

My Name Is Yoon by Helen Recorvits and Gabi Swiatkowska (Farrar, Straus & Giroux, 2003). Ages 4–8.

Peacebound Trains by Haemi Balgassi, illustrated by Chris Soentpiet (Clarion, 1996). Ages 7 & up.

The Korean Cinderella by Shirley Climo, illustrated by Ruth Heller (Harper Collins, 1993). Ages 5–9.

Korean Children's Favorite Stories by Kim So-Un, illustrated by Jeong Kyoung-Sim (Tuttle Publishing, 2004). Ages 5–12.

Sixteen Years in Sixteen Seconds by Paula Yoo, illustrated by Dom Lee (Lee & Low, 2005). Ages 5–10.

A Year of Impossible Goodbyes by Sook Nyul Choi (Yearling, 1993). Ages 10 & up.

Growing Up in a Korean Kitchen: A Cookbook, by Hi Soo Shin Hepinstall (Ten Speed Press, 2001). Ages 12 & up.

Asian Kites by Wayne Hosking (Tuttle Publishing, 2004). Ages 10 & up.

Finding My Voice by Marie Lee (Harperteen, 2001). Ages 12 & up.

A Step from Heaven by An Na (Front Street, 2001). Ages 10 & up.

The Legend of Hong Kil Dong: The Robin Hood of Korea by Annie Sibley O'Brien (Charlesbridge Publishing, 2008). Ages 8–12.

The Kite Fighters by Linda Sue Park (Yearling, 2002). Ages 9–12.

A Single Shard by Linda Sue Park (Clarion, 2001). Ages 10 & up.

When My Name Was Keoko, by Linda Sue Park (Yearling, 2005). Ages 10 & up.

For more good books about Koreans, Korean-Americans or Asian topics, visit:

http://www.cynthialeitichsmith.com/lit_resources/diversity/asian_am/korean.html

http://www.papertigers.org

Index